LEGENDARY PLACES

Contents

Camelot	2
Atlantis	10
Secrets in Stone	18
The Boy Who Flew Too High	26

CAMELOT

Written by Susan Brocker
Illustrated by John Ewing

For many years,
people have told stories about a castle
called Camelot (*KAM uh lot*).
They say King Arthur lived at Camelot.
He was a great king.

King Arthur had a magic sword
called Excalibur (*ex KAL ih burr*).
It had lots of jewels on it
and it could not break.
People say that King Arthur could not
be hurt if he held Excalibur.

There was a big, round table in the castle.
Brave men called knights (*nites*) sat at the Round Table.
They planned battles there.

A queen named
Guinevere (*GWIN uh veer*)
lived in the castle.
She was kind and beautiful.
All the people loved her.

What brave things do people do these days?

Sir Lancelot (*LANS uh lot*)
loved Queen Guinevere, too.
He was the bravest knight of all.
He fought big dragons and giants.
He won lots of battles.

A wise man lived in the castle.
His name was Merlin (*MUR lin*).
He used magic to help the King.

But there was a bad knight in the castle.
His name was Mordred (*MORE dred*).
He wanted to be the king.
He hated King Arthur.
He got the knights to fight each other.
In the end, the kingdom was destroyed.

Was Camelot a real place? Some people think that Camelot was in a town in the west of England. But no one knows for sure.

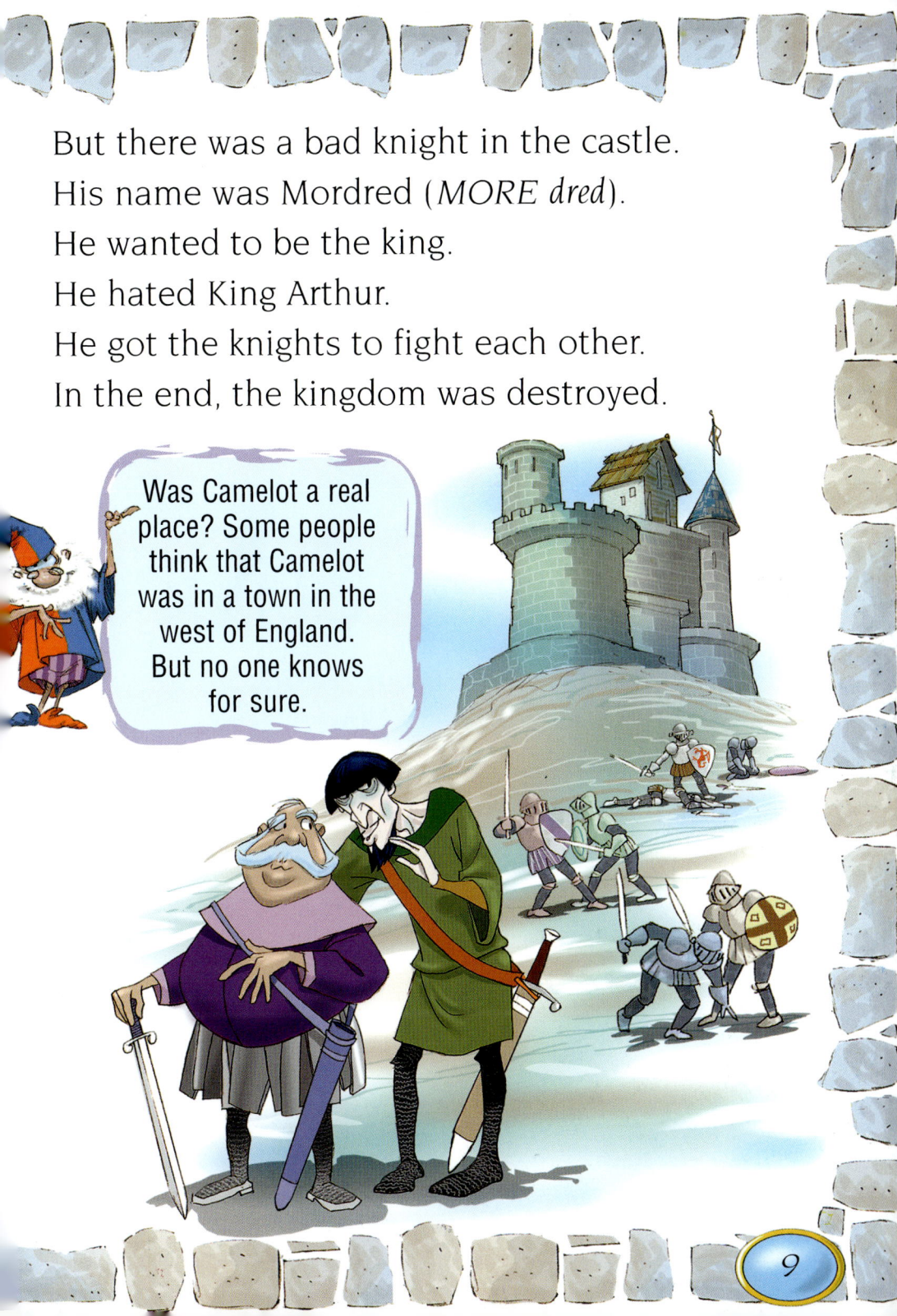

ATLANTIS

FACT OR FICTION?

Written by Susan Brocker
Illustrated by Xiangyi Mo
and Jingwen Wang

People say that there once was
a place called Atlantis (*at LAN tiss*).

They say that Atlantis was a big island.
It had lots of trees and flowers.
It had lots of birds and other animals.
The people had lots to eat and drink.
They were very happy on Atlantis.

The city on Atlantis was made out of silver, gold, and copper. It shone in the sun.

At the top of a mountain
was a big temple
for the god of the sea.
His name was Poseidon (*pohs I don*).

Poseidon became angry
that the people were fighting.
He made the sea rise up.
And Atlantis sank down into the sea.

Santorini today

Today the island is called Santorini (*SAN tor ee nee*).

Was Atlantis real? Some people think so.

Some people think that an island near Greece (*greese*) may have been Atlantis.

A mountain on the island erupted a long time ago. Much of the island sank beneath the sea.

Secrets in Stone

Written by Susan Brocker
Illustrated by Helen Humphries

Pyramid of King Zoser

Long ago, people in Egypt (*EE jipt*) made a pyramid (*PIRR ah mid*) for their king.

Secret passages led to a room in the pyramid. When the king died, they put his coffin in the room.

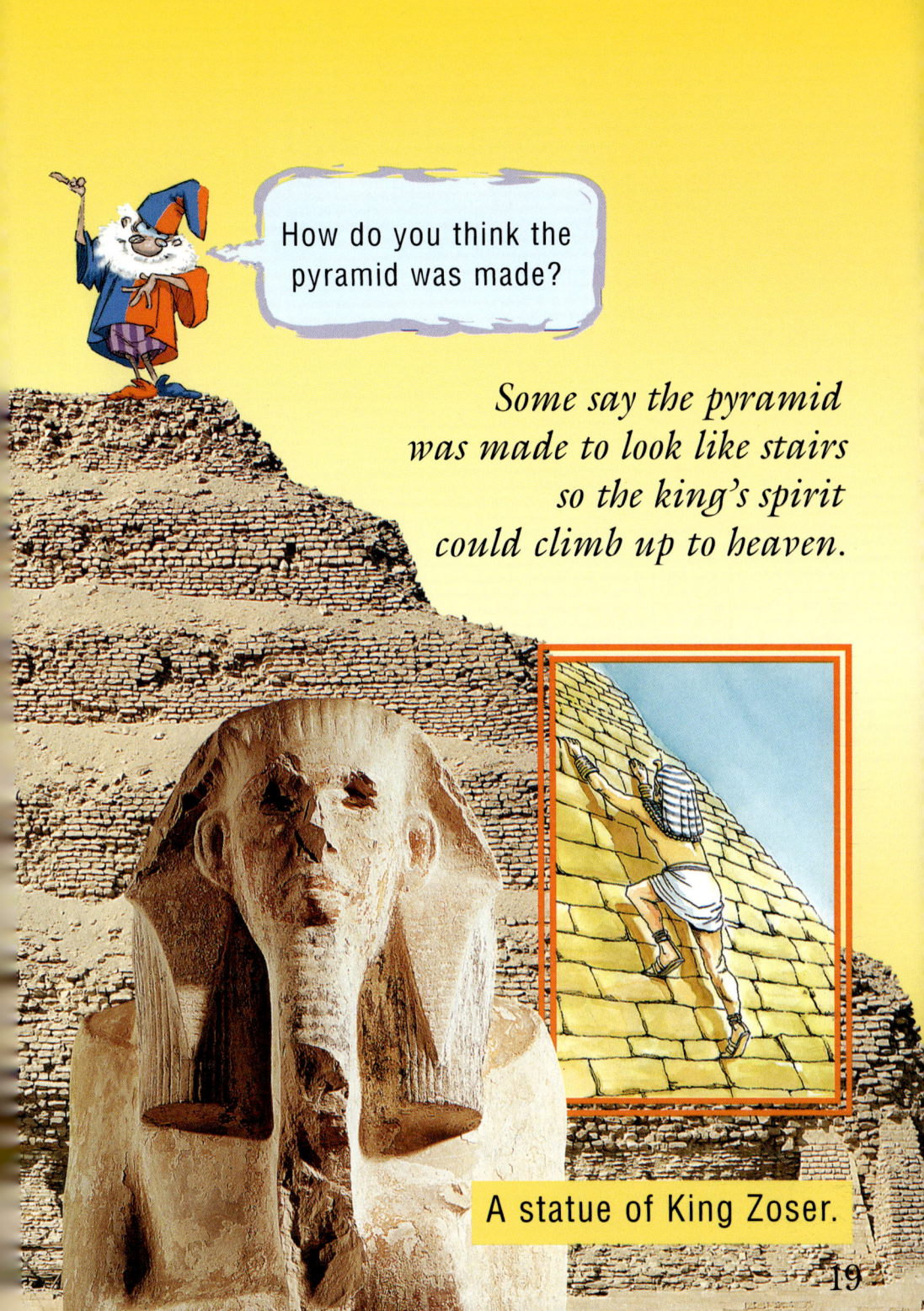

Tomb of Clay Soldiers

In 1974, people found the burial place of a Chinese emperor. With him, they found an army of soldiers made of clay.

There are rows and rows of soldiers. Each soldier is the size of a person. Each soldier has a different face.

Some soldiers have spears. Some soldiers have bows and arrows. Some soldiers have horses pulling chariots.

The soldiers were buried with the emperor. Some say the soldiers were made to protect the emperor after he died.

Chichén Itzá

Long ago,
Chichén Itzá
(*chee CHAN eet SA*)
was a great city.
You can still see the ruins
of temples and palaces there.
You can even see an old ball court!

One building is a round tower.
It is called the snail shell.
Some say the tower
was used to look at the stars.
They say looking at the stars helped
the people make the first calendar.

PALACE OF KNOSSOS

The palace of Knossos (*NOH suss*) was buried under the ground for many years. In 1900, a man named Arthur Evans began to dig it out. The palace has many rooms. It is like a maze. The walls have drawings of bulls.

Some say the palace was the home of King Minos. People used to tell stories about King Minos. Was he real? Or not?

The BOY Who Flew Too High

A Greek myth
retold by
Elizabeth Hookings

Illustrated by David Elliot

King Minos (*MY nos*) lived on an island near Greece. He had a monster called the Minotaur (*MIN ah tawr*). It was half man and half bull. It liked to eat people.

King Minos was looking for a place to hide his monster.

Some people think that King Minos lived in the palace of Knossos on the island of Crete.

He asked a man named
Daedalus (*DED uh luss*)
to help him.

Daedalus made a big maze for the Minotaur.
King Minos shut people in the maze.
The people couldn't find their way
out of the maze,
and the Minotaur ate them.

Daedalus was sorry that he had helped the bad King Minos. So he worked out a way to help a man named Theseus (*THEE see us*) kill the Minotaur.

Can you find out any more about Theseus and his story?

King Minos was very angry with Daedalus.
He locked Daedalus and his son Icarus (*ICK ar us*)
in a high tower.

Daedalus saw birds flying near the tower.
He got some feathers
and put them together with wax and thread.
He made four big wings,
so that he and Icarus could fly away.

"Don't fly too near the sun,"
Daedalus told Icarus.
"If you do,
the sun will melt the wax in your wings."

Daedalus and Icarus
flew up into the blue sky.
At first, Icarus stayed near his father.
But flying was fun!
He flew higher and higher.

"Come back," called Daedalus.
"You are too high!"

But Icarus did not hear his father.
The sun started to melt the wax.
The feathers started to fall.
Icarus flapped his arms quickly,
but his wings were gone.
Icarus fell down into the sea.

Index

Atlantis	10–17	Knossos, palace of	24–25, 26
Camelot	2–9	Lancelot	7
Chichén Itzá	22–23		
		Merlin	8
		Minotaur, the	26–28
Daedalus	26–31	Mordred	9
Excalibur	2–3	Poseidon	13, 15
		pyramid	18–19
Guinevere	6–7		
		Round Table, the	4–5
Icarus	29–31		
		Santorini	16–17
King Arthur	2–3, 8–9		
King Minos	24–25, 26–29	Theseus	28
King Zoser	18–19	tomb of clay soldiers	20–21
knights	5, 7, 9		